Things You'll Learn If You Live Long Enough

So You May As Well Know Now

D1512249

Great Quotations Publishing Company
Glendale Heights, Illinois

Compiled by Peggy Schaffer

© 1992 Great Quotations Publishing Company

Published in the United States by

Great Quotations Publishing Co.
1967 Quincy Court
Glendale Heights, Illinois   60139

Printed in Hong Kong
ISBN: 1-56245-054-9

The person who knows everything
has a lot to learn.

There is only one thing about which I am certain, and that is that there is very little about which one can be certain.

— *W. Somerset Maugham*

No man can think clearly
when his fists are clenched.

— *George Jean Nathan*

If you want a place in the sun,
prepare to put up with a few blisters.

— *Abigail Van Buren*

Experience teaches you to recognize a
mistake when you've made it again.

Good judgment comes from experience,
and experience comes from bad judgment.

— Barry LePatner

The trouble with using experience as a guide
is that the final exam often comes first and
then the lesson.

It's not what we don't know that hurts, it's what we know that ain't so.

— *Will Rogers*

When in doubt, duck.

— Malcolm Forbes

A friend in need,
is a friend to dodge.

Nothing is impossible for the man who
doesn't have to do it himself.

— *A. H. Weiler*

If you can't laugh at yourself, make fun of
other people.

— Bobby Slaton

Never mistake motion for action.

— Ernest Hemingway

A man is known by the company he avoids.

Men who never get carried away should be.

— *Malcolm Forbes*

It takes two to speak the truth — one to
speak and another to hear.

— Henry David Thoreau

Nature has given us two ears
but only one mouth.

— *Benjamin Disraeli*

It is easier to stay out than get out.

— *Mark Twain*

Talk is cheap because
supply exceeds demand.

You can't steal second base and
keep one foot on first.

— An unnamed 60 year-old junior executive

Virtue is its own revenge.

— *E. Y. Harburg*

One of the symptoms of an approaching nervous breakdown is the belief that one's work is terribly important.

— *Bertrand Russell*

Three o'clock is always too late or too early
for anything you want to do.

— *Jean-Paul Sartre*

In many ways the saying
"Know thyself" is lacking.

Better to know other people.

— Menander

Only the shallow know themselves.

— *Oscar Wilde*

The school of hard knocks is an
accelerated curriculum.

— *Menander*

You might as well fall flat on your face as
lean over too far backward.

— *James Thurber*

To love oneself is the beginning of
a life-long romance.

— *Oscar Wilde*

Only the mediocre are always at their best.

— *Jean Giraudoux*

He who laughs, lasts.

— *Mary Pettibone Poole*

It is only possible to live happily ever after
on a day to day basis.

— *Mary Bonnano*

There is more to life than increasing speed.

— *Mahatma Gandhi*

Life is what happens while you are making
other plans.

— *John Lennon*

Never believe anything until it has been
officially denied.

— Claud Cockburn

God gave you two ears and one mouth . . .
so you should listen
twice as much as you talk.

There is no job so simple that it cannot be
done wrong.

Choose a job you love, and you will never
have to work a day in your life.

The person who marries for money usually
earns every penny of it.

Our words may hide our thoughts, but our
actions will reveal them.

It isn't what you know that counts, it's what
you think of in time.

The older you get, the tougher it is to lose weight, because your body and your fat have become friends.

There's nothing sweeter than the patter of little feet . . . going off to school.

Even if you're on the right track, you'll get
run over if you just sit there.

The person rowing the boat
seldom has time to rock it.

You don't have to brush all of your teeth —
only the ones you want to keep.

People who know the least
always argue the most.

You never have to explain
something you haven't said.

It is especially hard to work for money
you've already spent for something
you didn't need.

Experts don't know either.

I cannot give you a formula for success, but I
can give you the formula for failure:
try to please everybody.

The best way to appreciate your job is to imagine yourself without one.

Marriage is compromise.

The Golden Rule:

He who has the gold makes the rules.

Rule of Success:

Trust only those who stand to lose as much
as you when things go wrong.

Age doesn't always bring wisdom, sometimes age comes alone.

Before you have an argument with your
boss, take a good look at both sides — his
side and the outside.

"Average but works hard,"
beats "brilliant but lazy."

Be yourself. Who else is better qualified?

After all is said and done,
more is said than done.

If you are going to stand on thin ice, you
might as well dance.

Going to college won't guarantee you a job,
but it will give you four years to
worry about getting one.

Never go to a doctor whose
office plants have died.

Being right doesn't count until the right
people know you're right.

Committee work is like a soft chair — easy to get into, but hard to get out of.

Be kind to your parents. After sending you through college, you're all they have left.

If people listened to themselves more often,
they would talk less.

Money won't buy happiness, but it will pay
the salaries of a large research staff to study
the problem.

"I tried, but it didn't work"
is a lot better than
"I wish I'd tried."

Everybody makes a very bad mistake at least once a week.

The trouble with trouble is that it usually
starts out as fun.

When your head swells up,
your brain stops working.

All children are born with a hearing
problem. They can hear everyone
but their mother.

Few people travel the road to success
without a puncture or two.

Get your facts first, then you can distort them as you please.

— *Mark Twain*

Never mistake endurance for hospitality.

Never give a party if you will be the most
interesting person there.

— *Mickey Friedman*

The best thing about a cocktail party
is being asked to it.

— *Gerald Nachman*

There are very few people who don't become
more interesting when they stop talking.

Nothing matters very much,
and few things matter at all.

— Arthur Balfour

Idealism is what precedes experience;
cynicism is what follows.

— *David Wolfe*

The secret of staying young is
to live honestly,
eat slowly,
and lie about your age.

— *Lucille Ball*

Remember, one good turn gets the blanket!

More marriages might survive if the partners
realized that sometimes the
better comes after the worse.

— Doug Larson

In prosperity, our friends know us;
in adversity, we know our friends.

— *John Churton Collins*

People need responsibility.
They resist assuming it, but
they cannot get along without it.

— *John Steinbeck*

The reward for work well done is the
opportunity to do more.

— *Jonas Salk, M.D.*

If you haven't any charity in your heart, you
have the worst kind of heart trouble.

— *Bob Hope*

Necessity is the mother of taking chances.

— *Mark Twain*

Don't aim for success if you want it; just do
what you love and believe in,
and it will come naturally.

— *David Frost*

People generally quarrel
because they cannot argue.

— *G. K. Chesterton*

The government deficit is the difference
between the amount of money the
government spends and the amount it has the
nerve to collect.

— *Sam Ewing*

Live so that your friends can defend you but
never have to.

— *Arnold H. Glasow*

Use soft words and hard arguments.

— *English Proverb*

Trust in God and *do* something.

— *Mary Lyon*

The more sympathy you give,
the less you need.

— *Malcolm S. Forbes*

Opportunity's favorite disguise is trouble.

— *Frank Tyger*

The surest way to lose a friend is to tell him
something for his own good.

— Sid Ascher

Don't lean over backward so far that you fall
flat on your face.

— *Ben H. Bagdikian*

It takes as much courage to have tried and failed as it does to have tried and succeeded.

— *Anne Morrow Lindbergh*

Nothing in fine print is ever good news.

— Andy Rooney

Ability will never catch up
with the demand for it.

— *Malcolm S. Forbes*

The past should be a springboard,
not a hammock.

— Ivern Ball

Reason deceives us;
conscience, never.

— *Jean Jacques Rosseau*

Everyone complains of his memory,
and nobody complains of his judgment.

— La Rochefoucauld

Blessed is the person who is too busy to
worry in the daytime and
too sleepy to worry at night.

— Leo Aikman

Luck never gives;
it only lends.

— Swedish Proverb

The only way to make a man trustworthy
is to trust him.

— *Henry L. Stimson*

Friends come and go,
but enemies accumulate.

— *Thomas F. Jones, Jr.*

Information's pretty thin stuff unless mixed
with experience.

— *Clarence Day*

Accomplishments have no color.

— Leontyne Price

The difference between a hero and a coward
is one step sideways.

— Gene Hackman

A committee can make a decision that is
dumber than any of its members.

— *David Coblitz*

You're never a loser until you quit trying.

— *Mike Ditka*

Advice is what we ask for when we already
know the answer but wish we didn't.

— *Erica Jong*

You know you're old when you've lost all
your marvels.

— *Merry Browne*

Stop worrying about the potholes in the road
and celebrate the journey!

— *Barbara Hoffman*

Every private citizen has a public
responsibility.

— *Myra Janco Daniels*

Candor is a compliment; it implies equality.
It is how true friends talk.

— *Peggy Noonan*

Everything looks impossible for the people
who never try anything.

— *Jean-Louis Etienne*

Character is much easier kept
than recovered.

— *Thomas Paine*

The best remedy for a short temper
is a long walk.

— *Jacqueline Schiff*

If a man has common sense,
he has all the sense there is.

— *Sam Rayburn*

Wit has truth in it; wisecracking is simply
calisthenics with words.

— *Dorothy Parker*

Marriage should be a duet — when one
sings, the other claps.

— Joe Murray

We don't know who we are until
we see what we can do.

— *Martha Grimes*

There are times when silence
has the loudest voice.

— *Leroy Brownlow*

Sports serve society by providing vivid
examples of excellence.

— *George F. Will*

No one should be allowed to play the violin
until he has mastered it.

— Jim Fiebig

The ultimate test of a relationship is to
disagree but to hold hands.

— *Alexandra Penney*

Expect people to be better than they are;
it helps them to become better.
But don't be disappointed when they are not;
it helps them to keep trying.

— *Merry Browne*

Kindness consists in loving people more than
they deserve.

— *Joseph Joubert*

Preconceived notions are the locks on the door to wisdom.

— Merry Browne

Accomplishing the impossible means only
that the boss will add it
to your regular duties.

— Doug Larson

Whoever thinks marriage is a 50-50 proposition doesn't know the half of it.

— *Franklin P. Jones*

Speak the truth,
but leave immediately after.

Plenty of folks are so contrary that if they
fell into a river, they would insist upon
floating upstream.

— *Josh Billings*

Spring is nature's way of saying,
"Let's party!"

— *Robin Williams*

Laziness has many disguises.
Soon "winter doldrums"
will become "spring fever."

— *Bern Williams*

If you want anything said, ask a man.
If you want anything done, ask a woman.

— *Margaret Thatcher*

It costs a lot of money to die comfortably.

— *Samuel Butler*

A married couple that plays cards together is
just a fight that hasn't started yet.

— *George Burns*

Among the country's surpluses are wheat, corn, cotton and calories.

— *Morris Mandel*

The shortest recorded period of time lies between the minute you put some money away for a rainy day and the unexpected arrival of rain.

— *Jane Bryant Quinn*

People need responsibility.
They resist assuming it,
but they cannot get along without it.

— *John Steinbeck*

To be upset over what you don't have is to
waste what you do have.

— *Ken S. Keyes*

Rules are made for people who aren't willing
to make up their own.

— Chuck Yeager

The point of living and being an optimist, is
to be foolish enough to believe the best is yet
to come.

— *Peter Ustinov*

A man begins cutting his wisdom teeth the
first time he bites off more than he can chew.

— *Herb Caen*

The best way to win an argument is
to start off by being right.

— *Quentin Hogg*

The art of being wise is
knowing what to overlook.

— William James

Knowledge is power, if you know it about
the right person.

— *Ethel Watts Mumford*

For every credibility gap
there is a gullibility fill.

— *Richard Clopton*

A diplomat is a man who always remembers
a woman's birthday but
never remembers her age.

— Robert Frost

Express a mean opinion of yourself
occasionally; it will show your friends that
you know how to tell the truth.

— *Ed Howe*

Virtue is insufficient temptation.

— *George Bernard Shaw*

By working faithfully eight hours a day, you
may eventually get to be a boss and work
twelve hours a day.

— *Robert Frost*

The man who sees the consistency in things
is a wit; the man who sees the inconsistency
in things is a humorist.

— *G. K. Chesterton*

The trouble with being punctual is that there is no one there to appreciate it.

— *Franklin P. Jones*

Time wounds all heels.

— *Jane Ace*

Changing husbands is
only changing troubles.

— *Kathleen Norris*

Men are creatures with two legs
and eight hands.

— Jane Mansfield

Banks and riches are chains of gold,
but still chains.

— Edmund Ruffin

Hope is merely dissappointment deferred.

— W. Burton Baldry

A dress that zips up the back will bring a
husband and wife together.

— *James H. Boron*

Nonsense is good only because common
sense is so limited.

— *George Santayana*

WHAT TO DO IN CASE OF EMERGENCY:

1. Pick up your hat

2. Grab your coat

3. Leave your worries on the doorstep

4. Direct your feet to the
sunny side of the street.